PLEASE DON'T FLUSH

Poems with bad illustrations

Aggie Jaworska

I kinda love you tho

Sorry about last night,
For feeding you a large Big Mac meal
With a side of 12 chicken nuggets, 2 cheeseburgers and pie.
I know how it feels.

Sorry for that day in April
When I stripped you bare
And got Mark from IT whip you with a leather belt to Classic FM
It's not very fair.

Apologies for all the nights
When I was 21
And all I did was let friends down and snort cocaine off a hooker's ass
It's not what I planned.

I sometimes regret
What I did to you in school

When all I fed you was air, biscuits, dick and booze

That really wasn't cool.

I'm sorry

For making you look less,

When I made you sweat every day to 'Get Slim Quick' workout tape

I thought it was for the best.

I hope you can forgive me

For all these times

I hurt you repeatedly with a knife and a lit cigarette butt

It doesn't even sound fun.

Please accept my remorse

For trying so hard

To look like Jenna, the influencer from Instagram,

That I forgot who you are.

Soz about today morning

When I looked at you

And thought-- you're ugly as fuck, but in reality

You're the only one I've got.

All I want for my birthday is a big-booty ho

I have aged

Once or twice

But it's the first time in my life

I've been this old

You might think,

Wow, you little genius, you

But the truth is

I don't know what to do

My uncertainty is deeper

Than the grave I'm digging myself

By smoking cigarettes

& drinking booze

(This is especially true if your father recently died of this, too)

But then I can't drink as much as I used to

And the peer pressure still exists

Even when you're 30

You get bullied to death

For drinking like a pussy

For not manning up

For not having that tequila shot

For not standing up to your boss

For eating red meat

For not eating red meat

For not paying your bills on time

For living with your parents because times are fucking tough (ok boomer)

For World War Two

For Leonardo DiCaprio not winning the Globes (again)

For not wanting to donate a pound to charity (as your payday is 3 weeks away)

For liking R Kelly

For liking ale

For not wanting better lives for the whales

For every single fucking thing on Earth

Depresh

Isn't that a kick in the teeth

You wake up and do the best
You can do

You watch Ted talks before bed

Daily you carry the balloon which says HELP

Finish deadlines on time even though you're dead
Inside

You rescue puppy harts
For the League Against Cruel Sports

You never smoosh spiders with your slipper
But gently take them outside

You help the prejudiced and oppressed

Accept themselves

Put plastic carefully in designated bags

Cry at funerals, weddings and while slicing bread

Embrace other's flaws like they're your own

And still the bitch is back.

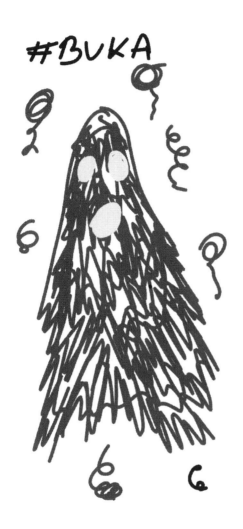

Fossils

I've learned that alcohol dependence

Could be hereditary

But what about dependence on dependence

I asked my mom

Because as an adult, I sometimes very much struggle

To wake up

To wash my hair

To bend my elbow

To smile and wave

To fix myself

Mirror Mirror

I've recently grown accustomed
To flatlines of my heart

Hardly anything is a thrill
Unless it's speed,
But speed makes me go fucking nuts
on sudoku for weeks.

Everything is more
Like a Chinese knock-off than real

I sometimes look at myself
and struggle
To associate me with me
As if I'm a tiny grain

In a kaleidoscope, and not much else

Your face and your voice

Are in deep-water monochrome

I need subtitles just to know

What you want from me

But I don't think I can read anymore.

Pottery

I'm a stupid clay vase
Like the ones they made in Ghost

And every day, I break into pieces
I'm all over the show
Until dawn

When I get a shitty instant glue
And glue myself together
Like an old shoe

I'm a stupid clay vase
And I'm glued through and through

Just to get through the day
Smile and wave,
Bend over and pray

That I don't break apart again.

I'm a stupid clay vase
Like the ones from Pompeii

And even though I glued myself
I fall apart comes dusk
So wobbly and frail.

I'm a stupid clay vase
Like the ones from Ancient Greece

So tired of gluing myself
All over again
Just so I can get through the day.

Untitled

What's wrong with me again

I'm tired of self-diagnosing

I wish someone could give this hell a name

WebMD

My armpits are sweaty again

I no longer know whether it's

Venlafaxine 150mg

Hodgkin's lymphoma

Lack of iron

Work stress

Meat sweats

Overactive thyroid

Early Menopause

Or I'm just scared of change.

Crisis team

Her name is Angela

She calls me every week

To make sure I'm still alive

She called me when I passed out

In my bathtub

After 3 bottles of wine

She called me back when

This guy broke my heart

And I decided I will hang on

She called me when I couldn't breathe

And even 54321 coping technique

Didn't quite work on me

Her name is Angela

And I know this is her job

To keep me alive

But somehow, I was almost sad

when she said after a month

Or maybe ten

I think you're now safe.

Sustenance

I'm fucking livid

Because you put tomatoes in the fridge

And excuse me, but who in their right

Likes tomatoes frigid

I'm angry

Yes, I'm angry, because you misplaced

My chia seeds, and this way I won't get

Enough protein in my meal replacement shake

You're out of your mind,

You put Aldi bag in the recycling bin

And you know fully well these are not yet

recycled, please check with your local council, for fuck's sake!

I can't even begin

To tell you how vexed I am

Because you messaged me while I was

In hatha yoga class, working hard and hot on my Zen

I'm furious.

Frankly, I'm slowly losing my shit

Cause you're playing COD online VERY LOUD with your friends

While I'm trying to read Rhonda's Secret & Deepak Chopra in peace

I'm absolutely fuming

Because Sharon told Karen at work that I'm a cheap slag

Which I overheard, and I can't deal with such

Toxic environment, so I literally packed my shit and left.

I'm so cross

I came home and cried for 2 hours straight

Even watching YouTube videos off baby red pandas,

Didn't quite help.

(I tried watching Pomeranian puppies, but that was also in vain)

I'm irate,

Because you found me on the floor

Crying into Starbucks chai latte

For no reason, and I haven't washed in 4 days

I'm sorry.

Because you kissed me on the forehead

And simply said--

Come on, baby, let me brush your hair.

Hibernate

I'm so full of love

I might burst in seams

But it's January

And it's cold

So I've put my love to sleep

Until spring comes

And the sadness thaws

Away

Bee's knees

I am fond of you

So much it hurts

My last kidney on the left

I am fond of your

Face and the way

You brush your ephemeral hair

I am fond of your

Chin and the way it points

Downwards

I am fond of your

Right elbow and your

Rather warm shoulder

I am fond of the

Fact you're convinced

That I think you're older

I am fond of your

Attempt to be brave

When you're, like, 12

It's admirable really

That you make my thoughts

Scatter like a swarm

Of bees

Bees

Bees

KNEES

Love hearts

Another night on Tinder
And my finger hurts
From swiping left and masturbation.

Another night on Tinder
My brain is about to blow
From all the sexual tension

If someone asks me
If I'm up too much again
I might shoot my phone into space.

Another night on Tinder
Pictures of drugged-up tigers
And rented cars

Another night on Tinder

I thought I found someone I like

But they are into Love Island and darts

Maybe I'm too picky,

But fuck knows why you think

It's ok to send me a photo of your dick.

Another night on Tinder

Maybe today

I'll find someone for sexy

 alien roleplay

Another night on Tinder

I don't understand

Why we talk all night

And then all day,

And then the convo dies

Leaving the stale taste in my mouth.

I'm on Tinder again

But CBA,

Everyone is just the same.

Returns not accepted

It was August in Paris,

To live was to search for Cortazar's grave

And for Oscar Wilde's goodbye kiss

For Sphinx, who sang him his memories.

In the shade of proud Notre Dame

We watched metro tickets rise and then land

Like some paper pigeons chased by a child.

Our feet were barely touching cobbled streets

Even Degas envied our light step

And painted us dancing in Versailles

Like fauns on a swan lake.

It was April in Paris,

And Edith Piaf told me to look through the pink glass,

But all I found was cold stone and grey dust

At the top of Montmartre.

We walked those cobbled streets

With your tired, blistered feet

A crippled pigeon greeted us in Notre Dame

With a ripped plastic bag in its beak.

Filled with hope, I took you to my favorite place,

But you rolled your hollow eyes at great Monet,

And said to me that he's just as dead as we.

Letter to my Grandmother

I read St Paul's letter to Corinthians and never understood,
How love can never fail
Until I looked at you two
How he sank in the chair, like a drowning man
Swallowed slowly by the cruel waves
Of despair. Blue veins on his worn hands,
Spider webs of time passed.

I never understood what through thick and thin meant.
Then I saw how he looked at your tired face
And saw a woman strong and brave.
Your heart, where your breast once was,
Undefeated and proud
Beat in perfect sync with his,
With every breath you draw.

I read poems about love. But I could never find

A single word that would ring as true

As my mother's words

That my grandfather won't eat, unless it's cooked by you.

So he wears his smile in the corners of his mouth

And nibbles on a stale slice of bread

Until you get your smile back.

Hurt

When I saw my mother washing my dad

In his cancer bed

I saw the apotheosis of love

Crowns made of thorns

If you were there you could smell

The sweet scent of agony

Mixed with sweat

And defeat

If you could see his once strong arm

Struggle to hold a joint

And black bile

On his teeth

If you could ask him how much it hurt

And he grabbed your hand

And said

Please don't go

If you could look him in the eye

And instead of comedy gold

See the dying light

Of dawn

If you could hear him cough and say

I really love you

And you wish you could stay

To soothe all his pain

Rubber dingy rapids

You look extremely handsome

When you put your arms around me

And I can feel your nails digging into my neck

You're so very clever

And talented

And you put all your talents into grabbing my face

I feel so much warmth

When I'm with you

Alone, where you can shout at me all you like

You're so spontaneous

We go on adventures

And when I look at someone else you call me a whore

You fill my soul

With precious moments

Of doubting myself whether I should've been born

You're so special

So special

I keep forgetting you were once addicted to brown

Everyone loves you

Even my friends

Didn't notice the bruise on my arms

We are both into fitness

We run together

But I can never run fast enough from you

Selfie

You didn't like my new Instagram post

But why

My mouth was open wide
Like a gaping Magikarp

The light was going wild
On my tits and face

The filter was California Dream
Which highlights the shape of my jaw

My eyebrows were so on fleek
And my bikini looked straight from High Street

But it was made by tired hands

Of child slavery in Hong Kong

My skin glowed through and through
Like a fucking moon

I bent my spine inwards and backwards
So my ass could look like 99 balloons

And all your mates liked it
With flames emojis and shit

I even got paid 20p
For holding a box of detox tea

It gave me incredible shits the next day

The sky and sea looked so clear
You would think I was in Bali

But I was in Clacton-on-Sea

Tomatoes

She's getting fondled on the dancefloor

But her last train to Chichester

Is leaving in ten

She's getting fondled on the dancefloor

But she knows she forgot to

Put her lunchbox in the dishwasher

She's getting fondled on the dancefloor

But the auction she follows on eBay

Ends in 4 hours

She's getting fondled on the dancefloor

But her right little toe is blistered

And it hurts like a bitch

She's getting fondled on the dancefloor

But her direct debit to Netflix

Is coming out tomorrow

She's getting fondled on the dancefloor

But she just remembered

She left a tomato soup on the stove

She's getting fondled on the dancefloor

But the current situation in Syria

Is troubling her

She was getting fondled on the dancefloor

But then she grabbed and broke his hand

In half, and he bled

He bled all over the dancefloor

But next day everyone said

She asked for it with her tiny dress

Wet Wet Wet

I had a dream about Lucy again

Her hard nipples were

poking through my eyes

Her jaw was tight

from drugs

Her hand was softer

then any man's

I could smell her pussy for five days

After she came on my face

You cheated on me with my best friend

And now I wonder

Were her lips sweeter than a box of quality street

Was her ass firm as a peach

Was her voice better than my hopeless

Squeak?

I also wonder

Was she as wild as a tramp on Jeremy Kyle?

Could she run more than five miles

Was it her smile?

I wanted to ask you so bad

Was she better than me in bed?

Was her touch as addictive as meth

Or was it the way she was the best

At literally everything else

I now often wonder will I ever be

Enough to feed

Any man I meet.

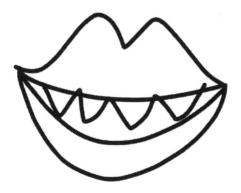

Clam

I was touched by a wrong man

He never asked permission

To please

He never took me to dinner

To tell me about his family shit

He never bought me a drink

To celebrate my Math's grades

He pried me open with his finger

Like a market clam

Will I now forever feel like a bag of flesh?

I was touched by a wrong man

He never asked permission

To laugh

And tell his friends, what a catch

And tell them everything about

The clam

Sad pandas

My bacon bap

Was very carefully packed

By Janice from the caf

Janice made sure

Every inch of my bap

Has been secured

But we are in England

And while country views are nice

It fucking rains

All the time

The train is late

Again

Why did I wear trainers

What's wrong with me today

I was happy once

But that was before

My bacon bap got soaked

In this everlasting rain

#PROTECT
BACON

Bonus content

I wonder if it's true what they say

About you and me

That things always die

And they're hardly ever built to last

Like an Ikea Kallax shelf

My biggest wish once was to

Swim in hot tubs

And drink mojitos

With colorful umbrellas in them

But alas I was wrong

Because anywhere I go

without you

s an apocalyptic

Empty shithole of a desert from Fallout 4

And not even the best

Fucking quest would not

make my life as big of an adventure

As when you're my Player Two

And I know people say

Loving is for the dumb

But they have no clue

That me and you

Make the best game in the world.

Burn

My only wish

My only desire

Was to put out that fire

That burnt through me

Like hell's 10th circle

Bright and blue

I thought I was to

Stop dreaming about

Unobtainable things

But then I learnt

That this fire

Was the only thing that was left

Of me.

Sweaty bed

The sheets cling to me
Like they're part of my skin

My hair grows into
The ground like branches

Like a weeping tree

The dirt under my nails
Doritos dust and dead skin

As I scratch myself till I bleed

tching to live

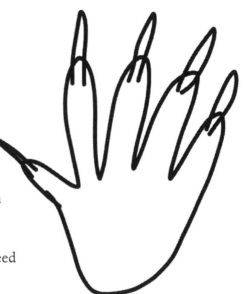

There was

A pretty big hole in her heart,

Ragged and rough.

She bought soil in Homebase

Plucked seeds from her throat

And planted flowers

To fill this hole

With life.

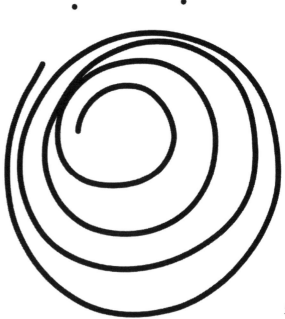

5

It's been ringing

Like this for hours

Ears are vibrating

Flashing light

                                                            Ring ring ring

He calls

They call

You call

I'm not here

I never listen to my voicemails

Out of fear.

HA HA
HAA

#newyearnewme

My New Year's resolution is to learn how to breathe

To learn how to count from 1 to 3

And then release

Perhaps my other one should be

Not to freak out on trains

Just chill

(or perhaps National Rail should sort their shit, but hey)

My next year's resolution is to finish my book

Kick the poet's block

In metaphorical cock

I would very much like in the New Year

To be able to run 5k

Without dying on the way

I always wanted to help homeless

But I'm too selfish

And rather play Candy Crush then make changes

In the New Year, I'd like to see

If I can make kale taste better

Than a dog's pee

I very much wish to be able to concentrate

For longer than Dory in Finding Nemo

But I get distracted by documentaries about pedos

Or maybe in the New Year

All I should really do is to be

kinder to myself

And everything else will fall into place.

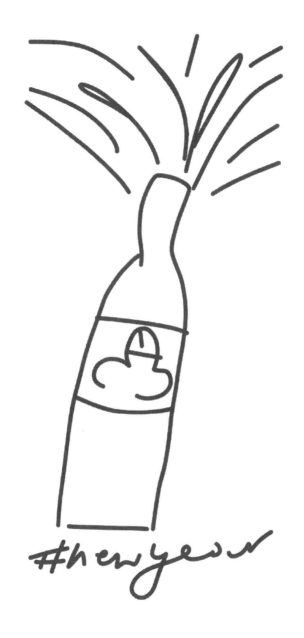

#newyear

Printed in Great Britain
by Amazon

36484294R00038